FOREST BOOKS

SNOW AND SUMMERS

SOLVEIG VON SCHOULTZ was born in 1907 in the coastal town of Porvoo in Finland. She was the youngest child of the Segerstråle family who were all artistically gifted. She is now the undisputed grande dame of Finland-Swedish literature, having published some thirty books ranging from poetry, short stories and other prose to plays for radio, television and the stage. Her work has been translated into eleven languages and she has won numerous literary prizes from her native Finland and from Sweden. In 1980 she received the Pro Finlandia Medal and in 1986 she was awarded an honorary doctorate from Helsinki University.

ANNE BORN is a poet, translator and historian. Her last translation for Forest Books was Bo Carpelan's *Room Without Walls.*.

A companion volume to this book is *Heartwork*, selected short stories by Solveig von Schoultz translated by Marlaine Delargy and Joan Tate, also published by Forest Books.

SNOW
AND
SUMMERS

Solveig von Schoultz

SNOW
AND
SUMMERS
(Poems 1940–1989)

by

SOLVEIG VON SCHOULTZ

translated from the Swedish
by
ANNE BORN

FOREST BOOKS
LONDON ☆ 1989☆ BOSTON

Published by
FOREST BOOKS

20 Forest View, Chingford, London E4 7AY, U.K.
PO Box 438, Wayland, MA 01778, U.S.A.

First published 1989

Typeset in Great Britain by Cover to Cover, Cambridge
Printed in Great Britain by BPCC Wheatons Ltd, Exeter

Translations © Anne Born
Original poems © Solveig von Schoultz
Cover design © Anders Carpelan
Introduction © Bo Carpelan
Photograph © Evy Nickström

British Library Cataloguing in Publication Data:
Schoultz, Solveig von, 1907—
Snow and summers: selected poems 1940–1989
I. Title   II. Born, Anne
839.7'172

ISBN 0–948259–52–3

FOREST BOOKS gratefully acknowledge the generous financial
support of the Finland-Swedish Cultural Foundation,
the Arts Council of Great Britain
and sponsorship from PAULIG LTD, Helsinki

PAULIG

We would also like to thank Jeremy Parsons for his help,
encouragement and enthusiasm in every aspect of the project.

Contents

Solveig von Schoultz

S olveig von Schoultz is the undisputed grande dame of
Finland-Swedish literature. During almost sixty years'
activity as a writer, she has published some thirty books
and her work has ranged across a broad spectrum from
poetry, short stories and other prose, to plays for radio,
television and the stage. In 1988 the Swedish publishers Bra
Lyrik issued a definitive edition of the poems she wanted
left for posterity. Translations of her writings have appeared
in Chinese, Danish, English, Finnish, French, German,
Gujarati, Hungarian, Norwegian, Russian and Spanish.

Born in 1907 in the coastal town of Porvoo, she was the
youngest of eight children of Albert Segerstråle, a theology
teacher, and his wife Hanna Frosterus-Segerstråle, the
painter. In 1930, while working as a primary school teacher,
she married Sven von Schoultz and her first book 'Petra
and the Silver Monkey' appeared two years later. With
'December' (1937) she began a series of semi-autobiographical
works which continued with 'Ansa and Conscience' (1954)
and 'There You Stand' (1973). In the two later volumes she
recreates with exceptional vividness and immediacy the
thoughts and feelings of a young girl as she passes from the
ages of ten to sixteen.

The birth of her two daughters Ursula and Barbara in
1934 and 1936 was to provide the material for 'The Seven
Days' (1942), an affectionate and minutely observed record
of the first seven years in her daughters' development; this
work has attained the status of a classic and is still considered
a standard work on the mother-child relationship and on
the upbringing of children. In 1978 she attempted to come
to terms with her feelings about her own mother in 'Portrait
of Hanna', which is also a portrait of an age and a chapter in

women's history. However, her most enduring achievement is probably the thirteen volumes of poetry she published between 1940–89 and her seven collections of short stories (1947–84).

Solveig von Schoultz was a member of the generation that followed the Finland-Swedish modernists of the 1920s and she can be said to have inherited their mantle, though with her own style and subject matter. Both Gunnar Björling and Rabbe Enckell were friends and their uncompromising attitude towards their work made a deep impression, as did Rilke and J.D. Salinger.

It has been noted that 'she gives voice to a feminine sense of life, to earth, sun, water and trees, conceived as symbols for all that is creative and growing'. Whether in poetry or prose, her response has been fundamentally that of a poet in that she has sought to capture the essence of an experience, situation or state of mind, often through symbol and metaphor. In her short stories, her prime concern has been with the inner life of her characters, with the possibilities for self-knowledge and growth within a person and a relationship. She is a master at revealing 'the hidden drama of the everyday' by using a simple episode to lay before the reader a whole life-situation in the space of a few pages. For her a short story is ideally 'like a waterdrop that reflects the whole of existence'. Although her writings do not fight shy of social problems, she has never been a militant feminist, preferring to concentrate on how it feels and what it is like to be a woman (or, more generally, a human being) at all stages of life. She has, however, had the satisfaction of seeing many of her early ideas taken up by later generations and given back to her renewed.

As she has grown older, her work has gained in economy, simplicity and directness. She has tirelessly honed and refined her language until it has become 'as clear and unobtrusive as a window-pane'. This is reflected in the fact that dialogue has all but replaced description in her short stories, and by her growing interest in drama. It has rightly been said that the amalgam at the core of her work is 'the will to observe and the desire to understand' and her short stories are distinguished by her generosity towards her characters and the sympathetic, loving distance she keeps from them.

Since 1961 Solveig von Schoultz has been married to the leading Finnish composer Erik Bergman who has made several settings of her poems. She has received numerous literary prizes both from her native Finland and from Sweden and her achievements as a writer have also been recognised by the Pro Finlandia Medal (1980) and an honorary doctorate from Helsinki University (1986).

Introduction
The Tree of Life,
in Darkness and Light

Solveig von Schoultz's first collection, *My Hour* (1940) includes the poem 'The mute trees.' In contrast to the joyful blossoming of spring, to new birch leaves and flowering cherry trees are the apple trees: 'they recall only icy cold,/chill dark that gripped through endless nights/when the young heart was smothered.' The poem is strongly constructed both in form and content: the contrast between the beauty of spring and the consciousness of 'shrivelled bark, dead hearts' demands the restraint of emotion. Yet the poem holds a rich palette of visual impressions despite the dominance of black and white. From the start Solveig von Schoultz speaks with her own voice. Intense emotion is waiting, hidden in the birch trees' passion and the cherries' indifference. The time is dark and demands its sacrifices. And yet, paradoxically: what seems dead blooms in spite of everything, what flowers will be numbed by winter. Existence is not either–or, it is both–and, it is 'blessed unease' and serene listening, it is doubt and decisiveness, wind and sun.

In Solveig von Schoultz's fourth collection, *Nocturnal meadow* (1949), the tree in the poem 'Lament for an alder' is a 'bearer of secrets', a symbol of liberty in the mysterious communication of direct experience. The four elements are present in this poetry with its religious overtones. The alder becomes a 'mediator' and when the tree is no longer there, the observer is left unprotected. Following 'Lament for an alder' is the poem 'Felled tree'; its silence is the silence of something cut off. What has been seen and closely observed is full of portents: of disintegration, of warning, the eternal symbols of life and death. But the tree is also (in the poem

'The Tree') an image of masculine strength — 'How could this tree then understand a plant?/A plant whose life held but one brief summer?' Hard and soft, eternal and transient are parts of a whole in which unease can be sunlit and serenity turn towards darkness.

The well-known poem 'Tree' with its refrain 'There's nothing for it but to be more tree' is in *Everything happens now* (1952). It exhibits deeper insight into both theme and inner movement: 'the tree's direction:/deeper down' is the demand made on the poet. And to the question 'Can a tree that loves the gale become a gale?' she replies with awareness of universal dynamic changes, of the forces that fuse in the tree's form and are at the same time search, longing, departure. The tree absorbs nourishment from both light and darkness and is 'always in motion.' The mute tree, the dead tree, the felled tree are gone and a dark shadowy tree now stands as an image of life's dynamic transitions. There is always time for change.

In the poem 'The wind' from *The net* (1956) the time for change has come and the tree is now merely an object, the subject of the adult wind's love for 'thousands of trees.' The wind's maturity is newly gained, it gives the poem a freer, less laborious, released form, it 'fulfils its heart on its own/ stronger/grizzled/salt.' The dreams of the intercessor, perhaps slightly romantically vague and faintly echoing Södergran, the striving to go 'deeper down' into the dark earth, give way to a stronger aspiration — for the dynamic movements of the wind that embrace everything and give fresh salt to the language. And new insights into the importance of being able to linger: 'Take care not to travel too fast,/to believe in another valley/a larger one you've heard of/there is no other/not for you/hold back/print each leaf in memory.' The valley with its trees 'bears the name of Love' and is here and now, real, no dream. The woman who walks through the tangibly expressive landscape of the poem is 'weather-beaten' and aware, her departure is not pain and dissolution but 'more/shining circles of immensity.'

A newly-born flexibility marks the poems in *The four flute players* (1975). Symbol has been replaced with observed image and this image is given graphic definition and wintry clarity in 'All trees wait for birds':

> When the light opens its eyes
> the landscape is new-fallen snow
> and fresh as frost
> no tracks to be seen
>
> not the faintest featherstitch of lies
> the shadow's a hungry blue
> and all trees wait for birds
> all unknown
> here is neither good nor bad
>   a mouse
>   scampers fearless across the sun.

There is freshness and compression here, and a lightness of touch resulting from the long practice of craftsmanship, of experience. Trees and birds have no name, not because they are nameless but because they do not need to be named: they exist, have a place in the landscape, in non-identity, they belong to all and to none, and freedom bears the name of mouse. The trees' waiting is like the stump's: hopeful. Serenity is present even in the inescapable: Solveig von Schoultz's poem is the poem of perception. One of the most significant poems — and most beautiful — in my view is 'Gone away':

> It's quite possible, when you sit in the sun
> to sit in the shade, see the rolling waves
> merely as glinting lies over the rocks
> only see hunger in gulls' yellow eyes
> autumn in the sun-dried grass at your feet.
> It's quite possible when you sit in the sun
> to have gone away, not answer to a call
> feel in your innermost room the grey hand
> close the windows.

Nothing can be added to this inescapability; what is said has the stamp and weight of finality. The great poem achieves this objective overview when with apparent effortlessness and without using special devices it imparts sun and shade, wind and innermost room, roots in earth and crown sweeping the sky in the same indivisible reality. The poet is (in the poem 'Siesta') 'perfectly free/to choose my domain' — with the inimitable addendum 'between three and four'. Von Schoultz chiefly concentrates on the gentle feminine world, the role of mother and child, so that her sense of humour is not always obvious; but to me the shaping power in this poem is clear.

Trees are present in the title of the collection published in 1980: *The sea sounds beyond the trees*. It sounds, and is also seen: for both poet and reader von Schoultz's poetry is an exercise in sense-sharpening. Now from the tree the bird's song is heard as a more profound portent of departure: joy and despair are close to each other, happiness and sadness too. It is November:

> Now life and death have gone their separate ways,
> Death is still strolling
> along the black leaves.
> Life has gone home
> to sleep in its roots.
> The fields breathe deeply
> and settle themselves.
> Darkness and rest. At last.

It is the winter tree that is apostrophised here, frost's tree of thought whose every branch extends contemplation 'more brittle and white/the closer to sky./Nothing hidden/not even birds/only the bare trunk/dark and real.' Thus what was once a carefully worked symbolic image built up of many nuances and substances has become an image no less complex but clearer, more concrete, direct and tangible: one is led to think of Helene Schjerfbeck's later paintings or of Käthe Kollwitz's graphic works (a portrait of Kollwitz appears in the collection *The waterhweel* (1986). See page 00.) What remains is 'the trunk', reality perceived. This also applies to the experience of personal identity. 'Five-finger exercise' — the remarkable and generous lyrical finale to *The sea sounds beyond the trees* — speaks of the 'I' which belongs to us all, [of] a 'silence and emptiness' waiting to be filled, [of] the perception that 'no day/[is] empty and 'in vain', that everything affects everything in the world of the present moment and in memories. I cannot imagine a more cogent summing up of almost fifty years of poetic creation.

The sincerity and smiling wisdom engendered by a lifetime of experience appears again in *The waterwheel* where trees — in accord with Solveig von Schoultz's later poems — 'are thinned out to graphite-grey streaks', where the giant pine bars the way 'with something that was more than icy silence': indeed, 'somethinhg more' is the result of the von Schoultz poem's concrete perception: a margin for the vision, the dream, the unknown. Solveig von Schoultz's poetry speaks with lasting strength of truths, abiding though paradoxical, seen and experienced through the whole spectrum from darkness to light, not dimmed but clearly illuminated in the poet's innermost room.

Bo Carpelan

from
My hour
(1940)

Min timme är kort

Den heliga oron slog på min port.

Jag har inte tid, jag bakar mitt bröd,
degen jäser, ugnen är röd.
Vänta, såsom du väntade förr.

Den heliga oron gick från min dörr.

Den heliga oron tog i mitt lås.

Träd mig ej nära, ett barn är fött,
det suger mitt blod, min märg, mitt kött.
Lämna mig ensam med min son.

Den heliga oron gick därifrån.

Den heliga oron stod i mitt hus.

Såg du ej skorstenens bråda rök?
Jag sopar min sjuka grannes kök.
Barnen gråter. Men tack att du kom.

Den heliga oron vände om.

Den heliga oron satt vid min säng.

O, är det du? Nu ä jag trött.
Jag skulle älskat dig ung eller dött.
Ville du något? Min timme är kort.

Den heliga oron gick gråtande bott.

My hour is brief

Blessed unease rattled my gate.

I haven't time, I'm baking bread,
the dough's rising, the oven red.
Wait, as you did before.

Blessed unease turned from my door.

Blessed unease lifted my latch.

Don't come closer, a child is born,
it sucks my blood, flesh, marrow from bone.
Leave me alone here with my son.

Blessed unease turned and was gone.

Blessed unease entered my house.

Didn't you see the chimney smoking?
I'm sweeping my sick neighbour's kitchen.
The kids are crying. But thanks for coming.

Blessed unease lingered in going.

Blessed unease sat by my bed.

Oh, is it you? I'm tired now.
I should have loved you and died young.
What do you want? My hour is brief.

Blessed unease left, bent with grief.

The mute trees

Speedwell and clover whisper around their feet,
the birches have forgotten everything, in love with
                                    their new leaves,
Indifferently cherries drop white petals on the hair
                                    of the passer-by
but the apple trees brood over memories
dark as their branches.

What do they care for the murmur of childish grass,
the grass that slept through bad times.
What's the prattle of new leaves to them,
jewels on trees who ought to know better
than to thank summer.

The apple trees' stiff branches bar the way,
fumble blindly: they see only blue snow,
shiver in the soft wind: they recall only icy cold,
chill dark that gripped through endless nights
when the young heart was smothered.

Who comforts roots that know ice lurks
far into summer, know shrivelled bark,
that dead hearts await green rashness?
Who hears the plaint in numb branches:
You remember? Remember? And you can bloom?

The water-butt

I love the eye
of the water-butt on the corner.
In the morning it laughs
when the aconites borrow its mirror
    and deck themselves out for the butterflies,
in the heat it is shadowy, aloof,
    talks softly to honeysuckle leaves,
plays sometimes with the children
    and ripples Lilliput waves for bark boats,
but not until night-time when children and
    grownups have gone,
does the eye really wake, widen,
clear and listen,
open to the dark above the pines
and take Aldebaran
into a cool embrace.

Wind and sun

If you're wind then I'm sun.
If you're an icy field with sleeping seeds
then I'm spring that wakes them with a kiss
and frees the captive powers of earth.
If you're only promise then I'm gift.
If you are thoughts then I am words.
If you're the sullen wind that slakes the flame
then I'm the spark that kindles it again.
If you're the lock, in rigid ornate mould,
then I hold the key here in my hands.

If you're hesitation, I am decision.

The newborn

Betrayed in that hour
when night ebbs, people die
and all distress lies naked,
my child wails.

A raw pain drifts about the room.
Part of me, barely torn away,
trembles its homelessness.

Now each nerve in my body answers,
the heart swells under my left breast,
stops beating.

From worlds of dark
echoes a wail, a wail:
a great strange bed,
a great strange space,
cold, full of dread,
endless.

What can I give you?
Nothing.
We are two.

Betrayed to life,
my child wails.
Each nerve in my body mutely wails.

30.XI.1939

Then even that day ended.
Our lantern's blue gleams
flickered over dark asphalt
empty as gutted homes.

Our feet crunched shattered glass
from windows' blinded eyes
cautious, as if from somewhere
there might come stricken cries.

But the street was already dead.
Pale wounded walls had bled,
stood with gashed eyes
where yesterday children played.

Smoke drifted past,
acrid, souring the air.
The window nearest our lantern
gaped dumb and bare.

Curtains stiff with soot.
A nightwind fingered them.
They lifted like black wings,
birds without a home.

from
Joy turned aside
(1943)

Prayer

Bread, stay in my hands.
Bestow life's warmth, divinely bounteous,
and let me lean my cheek to your rough bark,
trusty bread.

How good your brown fragrance:
grain sweetened in sun, dark granary, corn rustle.
Blood flowed into you from earth's womb,
ruddy bread.

Heathen women shaped you with invocations
and Christian crosses encircled your sacred encampment:
dark weapons were laid down at your glance,
man's bread.

Revered bread, you saw forebears arise,
you, born of soil, buried in soil and born again,
do not desert us in our last hour,
merciful bread.

Primeval mother

I saw the primeval mother:
she hurried round the corner in clumsy men's boots,
her jacket blowing round her hunched-up back.
Mud sucked at her heels
and her ragged dress flapped heavily round her legs.
She had no face, but an earth-coloured kerchief,
she rushed, simply rushed, with hanging arms,
along the street to the meat queue.

We'd seen her before in misfortunes,
that evening the last bread was broken
the morning cows lowed with bursting udders
the night frost struck the pale acres.
A thousand years of twilight brooded under her scarf
and raw grey worries dragged at her hems.
None knew what forests she'd come from
nor in what hiding-places agony seized her,
ancient agony curled up by the fire,
grey, with indrawn claws and yellow eyes,
agony that drove her out of the past,
bark-bread, hunger-silenced children, empty huts,
drove her blind and headlong
towards the meat-queue.

The butterfly

Every day a buttefly visits the boulder,
clips holes with bright wings in the gloom beneath the
pines,
seeks out the way to the sun with lanky antennae,
glides capriciously over the stonecroft tufts,
trembling clings to
the purple rose of a chive.
He sails sideways down
among a flock of laughing brown grasses.
So many kisses confuse him,
he hangs quivering with closed eyes,
the boulder's bright waves wash over him.

Suddenly he rises, renewed,
whirls recklessly, shining, a silver leaf
and rises, rises,
darling of clouds and winds,
rises to the rowan clusters
rocking close to heaven,
giddy flower.

A single minute

I hold a single minute in my hand:
a low island runs into green water.
Drops from reeds. A shining streak:
the shy grebe's sun-trail.
Worlds of giant clouds
gripped by an invisible hand
parting night-blue
from dove-grey and mist-grey.
Light breaks through. Who sinks
God's heart into green water?

August

The carefree scrap of fluff
shook out its fibres in bright silence
and floated out over little glittering waves,
long since forgotten by the seagull's wing
it rocked out into mother-of-pearl eternity
alone.

The carefree white cloud
rose above the rock's yellow grass,
lay on its back and glided out to sea
lazily, and watching the vanishing rocks,
dots in the unknown, began to sing to itself
alone.

The woman in the drifting boat
listened to the silence that rose from the water,
rested on her oars and forgot where she had come from,
forgot her name and stillness rose in her
shone in her, effaced her and reigned
alone.

The lover

My eyes want to kiss your face.
I have no power over my eyes.
They just want to kiss your face.
I flow towards you out of my eyes,
a fine heat trembles round your shoulders,
it slowly dissolves your contours
and I am there with you, your mouth
and everywhere around you —
I have no power over my eyes.

I sit with my hands in my lap,
I shan't touch you and I'll never speak.
But my eyes kiss your face,
I rise out of myself and no-one can stop me,
I flow out and I'm invisible,
I cannot stop this unfathomable flowing,
this dazzle that knows neither end nor beginning —
but when at last you turn your eyes towards me,
your unaware, questioning, stranger's eyes,
I sink myself back into my hands
and take up my place again under my eyelids.

Ageing woman

Now the little warm mouths have left my skin,
now I no longer meet men in my dreams,
now my blood's joy is a shrivelled autumn leaf,
now I have room for myself.

All the hard years have worn away my senses,
all the forgotten sorrows run out of my eyes,
something was there that nothing could wear out:
the thirst to understand.

I've dwindled, bent low over coarse hands.
But voices rise, too quiet for my ears,
I've caught a gleam from good and wicked eyes:
something awaits me.

Eternity, let me sit on your lowest threshold,
allow me, ignorant, to listen slowly,
be aware if light falls past me down to earth,
and help me understand.

from
Echo of a cry
(1946)

The park crones

Each autumn the park crones sprouted from the grass.
Their boots were black as birch roots,
red cackles fluttered in their aprons
and their deep purple dresses were earth's respite.
They bore summer's patience under their head scarves
but gales lived in their huge brooms.
Against brilliant October skies stood a pillar of leaves
worn, bitter, withered and furiously glad.

Under the park crones' feet all sickness turned to blight
and their rough footprints reeked of decay.
But when fog and chill swirled around bare boles
they lost their colour, grew grey and yellow,
glum as gravediggers and secretive as midwives,
brown as winter buds with surly defiance.

The hen-bird

Just like a woman, hesitant, restrained,
held fast within life's fair and downy years,
a mother who over low beds could bend
and quite forget to see the sun ascend,
she left the warmth and shelter of her home,
a nest too narrow now for her young ones.
She found a truth that she'd refused to own,
she found the summer was far gone, O far.

But yet her breast was still a soft song-night
and all her feathers glossy, smooth and sleek.
And suddenly she knew what life had meant:
a brief hot summer, woman, is still yours.
A brief hot summer. Quick. Far on the year.
And later? A journey, mysterious, in secret,
an early autumn, merciless and clear.

The lovers

I

When you stroked my hands
slowly, inside, silently, one at a time
something sprang up, a captive flock of birds.

And when your mouth took mine, sank into it,
blinding wings beat at my eyelids:
let me out, set me free. I must be free.

But when you kissed my breasts
buds quivered and grew, my skin found voice
and broke out in a cry, a soundless cry.

II

All around us soughed the world's night
where the hunter trod with his booming heel
and the hound with its desolate howl,
where arrows flew from unknown planets
and where the black gale drowned every cry.

But we lay stretched out on a bed of stars,
a bed of stars, and were afraid of nothing.
And as long as my face breathes its summer against
                                    your shoulder
and as long as your hand rests its peace upon my thigh,

as long as we inwardly listen with closed eyes,
inwards to each other, past longing or memory,
as long as our smiles flow together into the dark,
so long are we clasped within our shining trust
and no ill can touch us.

The leavetaking

The children slept, and her husband, when she went
soundlessly, barefoot, like a sleepwalker.
Her tenderness she laid beside him, a scent
of solace like a mute pressed lily of the valley
that holds June in itself well into autumn.
And while the light breathing of the children
rose around her just like clover winds
she softly laid her tears down with one,
her laughter with one, her song with another,
and stood and looked and did not dare to look
but stroked a curl away from the smallest brow
and hurried with closed eyes towards a door,
the door of night, a door that opened out
to where the moon waited, cold, clear, bold.
Now she had given away her very last mite.
Nothing was left to her except her body
and the agony in that body's resolve.
At the door, already gone from what had been,
she turned, looked back and knew what she had done.

The fist of necessity

Three times a day forced to the knees
by necessity's grubby-knuckled fist,
four times sunk in a black-speckled dazed confusion
while what's neglected throbs in an empty skull,
five times drained to the last dregs of endurance
while love runs out through fingertips,
six times driven away from the room with the secret
                                    flute,
seven times stamped down, seven times up again with
                            new defiance,
each night embraced by a sorrow sunk to the bottom,
cooled by dreams like windflowers, cast by the wayside,
woken by dawn with dark circles under the eyes —

And you think you can break me, life?

from
Nocturnal meadow
(1949)

Lament for an alder

Only when you'd gone did I see who you were,
bearer of secrets.
Through you water came to me
you let its brilliance shine through thousands of
little screens
calm came through you with smooth, milk-white discs
and coolness that hid itself in earth's grass.
You stood between me and the sun like a mediator,
you gave me rippling shadow while you drank.

Each morning your quivering diadem told me what
the heavens willed
each evening you asked me what the day had given
and at noon the willow warbler would rest on a little
broken twig.
Now you have gone the naked bay stares,
I search for shelter, who will give it me?
And where shall I rest my thoughts, on what bough?

Felled tree

Like a divorced woman
the crown rallies its leaves
capriciously fluttering
thinner-skinned than before
chattering away
shriller than before

(the fracture weeps freshness
runs sap)

like a wife
cut off from her root
from the earth's manhood
tremors from the dark
from night's nourishment
water's resting-place
the crown gathers its soughing
draws leaves around it for shelter

(no-one needs shelter now)

before it suddenly
lets go

falls silent.

The heart

We fed her corn, not much
but enough to keep her going,
she had water, a thimbleful
to remind her of the well-spring,
we opened the door just a crack
so the sky punched her in the eye
and we fixed a piece of mirror to her cage
so she could look straight into the cloud.
She sat quiet, wings quivering.

That's how she sang.

Vision

Alone at the edge of a lake
stands a woman
utterly dark
utterly tree
roots spread
under the peace of the downtrodden.

In her rough trunk
messages run, still young,
from what's below
from what's above
her eyes shine under the clouds.

She stretches out
veined hands,
little men sit there
bright little transparent men.
Curiously, in sorrow,
she sees their spry little sex,
their spry little mettle,
red sap of hate.
They hold spears in their hands.

Carefully she puts them down
to play among the roots.
Utterly dark
utterly tree
she washes her hands in the wind.

Woman cleaning fish

With my long brown arms
I hurl guts into the sea
wind and perch-scales fight for my neck
sea-grass coils round my toes
dead mouths yawn
— there! my quivering heart with white gobbets of fat
dive deep, a scream
— you omnivorous stomach that grinds anything and
everything
sway in shaggy seaweed
I shan't look at you
— you yellow bile, you insult to the sun
you stinking bitterness
may the stomach crab get you
eat your
intestines' wriggling excuses
stinking memories' cowardly constipation
— with my long arms
I hurl gulls' raucous laughter.
Tear shiny membranes
snort my blood, I will crunch and be rinsed
vomited out in scornful cold and salt-green:
neat white flesh and a few fierce spines.

The rain

The rain shook its hair out carelessly over the streets.
I stood in a doorway thinking of you.
The lamp whipped up thin threads of fire
before they plunged blindly to oblivion's foot.
Thus, lit by my heart
the darkness streamed out of you
past past

fallen into the dark.

The tree

Perhaps that was the difference: he was a tree.
He had the greatest thing: time to grow,
to turn his leaves to the sun, turn them down
to shelter the grass around his faithful feet.
He had time to wind his root around the stone
pondering, searching out his leisurely way,
time to harden, time to spread his crown
while distant summers waited in his bark.

How could this tree then understand a plant?
A plant whose life held but one brief summer?

from
Everything happens now
(1952)

You always thought

You always thought dull fields were radiant green.
Believed more good was in store for you.
That earth welcomed the thunder of your hooves.
That there was room for your shining mane.

The sun dwelt in your great body.
Your flanks shone with life's sweat.
Your muzzle was strength's tenderness
and mares fell silent at your call.

Unsuspicious one, what did you know of boundaries?
What did you know of envy's barbs,
of mean fences that tore at your leaping hooves?

No accusation in your mute eye.
Richly
your warm death runs out into the grass

your sun steams out of you
and your end is as your beginning:
trust.

Lost

Just before she lay down
before the lost one relinquished her body
she stood with closed eyes against a tree
and under blood-red eyelids
fell and fell like snowflakes
fell down the years towards a forbidden peace:
an old-fashioned sofa in a narrow room
the smell of clean linen, a red shawl
a bottle of cough mixture, a lump of sugar
a soft humming behind the doors of the stove
that shook out its northern lights over the floor
dangerous but held back by an infinite safety
and a soft humming behind the open door:
sleep, my child, and an infinite safety
a blood-red safety:
almost at home with God.

Lazarus

Three days he had lain wrapped in his decision
with a dark imprint on his headcloth:
eyelids; they had renounced everything
closed over smothered vanity,
nose: its haughty monument
to vanished memories of happy life,
behind the bitter lips, the dried tongue
regretting its waywardness here and there,
ears; a final lock
behind which he was himself at last
in a pit of amazed silence;
but mutest of all his hands
with brooding knuckles: all in vain.

Like an onion under layers of the past
one memory hibernated in his heart,
a little whitish sliver of dread,
but this too prepared itself for death
when, through the caves of silence
                              a blast reached him,
a trumpet of light and he answered with silence
and stiffened withdrawn in his shell

till the trembling struck him again
the close pulsing of strange light
and the sliver of dread swelled in his heart
and with his dead body Lazarus cried out No.

The commanding trumpet.
                              An intolerable pain
a violent light flooded his limbs
light strong as death, stiff bandages bursting —
                              Lazarus. Come forth.

Tree

There's nothing for it but to be more tree.
Make peace with the soil. The ever changeless soil.
Changeless: the stones.
The gravel changeless.
Forever nailed to this: immobility
Be moved in the tree's direction:
deeper down.

Can a tree that loves the gale become a gale?
A tree can do nothing but wear out its crown.
Be shaken by visions
shot through with burning cries.
The nailed-down tree roaring
born to tree
thrusts its longing inwards
in tree-form.

The dark-shadowed one grows broader. Broad,
the column pushes down, and with no fear of height
sings its leaf-heart greater towards the clouds.
Rest for all travellers
safety for birds and seeds
always in motion
deep in its innermost wood.

There's nothing for it but to be more tree.

The pike

Me?

I am the pike.
Yellow-ringed green and black:
tail-hard triumph.
To me all power is given.

Who are you?

I took your bait.
Its snare glitters within me.

Never think I regret it.
I wanted it. Took it.

True: it hurts
under my strong heart.
But rarely, dully.
What do you want? To play me?

Don't think you have me.
It's my whim to come when you call.
Now and then startle you
with sudden sly twists.

But away!
Away from your evil eye
in a whistling, whirling vortex
diving deep into night
— my playtime's shadow-clear hunting ground
my trembling small fry, my snapping jaws
my arrow-swift hissing will —

Strike.
Strike under my wild heart.
Is it death I've swallowed?

But take me alive?
Never.

June sauna

This is the body's bliss unmindful of age and sex:
to curl toes against a sooty wall
stripe back-skin against redhot bench
rolling shadows round stomach's pit

eyes dazzled by a window, tiny and furiously green
frayed spotted curtain
inquisitive nettle-crowd
gasp at the hissing alder whisk

draw blessed breath by the stones' steaming groan
drip guile from the skin
scoop innocence from the tub
be polished childlike, glossy wet

crawl in a glow away from the little soot-black island
chew wood-sorrel dreamily
ice-cold blueberry flowers
whistle to the stock-dove's weeping-song

and behind a bush pay your evening call.

Dream

A sudden beam of light
shone through all the skirts
round her body's dark core.
She threw them off hastily.
They rose like poppy petals
flew over the bed like white bells.
The man grabbed at them
buried his mouth in their cool submissiveness
dipped his face in her fleeting scent.
But she stood stripped
forgotten
by the bed.

Pain

You threw me off.
A rain of stones
struck my face and your fiery hooves
vanished.

I know you'll come back
trembling, sweating,
And I shall mount you:
my spurs thirst for your hide.
I'll mount you:
force down your mutiny between my knees
and we'll journey together
as one
in silent tight-reined steps
one for one.

The room by the river

The only calm is to break one's calm
to know when water stagnates, starts to smell.
The calmness of a windless shore is false
and the house of safety stands with shutters barred.

But give me this room of river-blue air
with walls that are still empty,
this bare floor of boards
leading towards a single point: the window,
open to the flow of water night and day.
Here all illusion will be washed away
in wicked little swirls
and day and night sluice away
small pieces of myself.
Until I'm bare and hard as the floor
                    by the river,
till what's makeshift lifts
like clouds of autumn finches,
till I stand open like a window
to the brown sun of change.

from
The net
(1956)

The well

Early in the morning I go to my well
sometimes so early that the pail fills with stars
sometimes in the night I go to my well
lift high the handle
                    lower the pail
down into invisible blackness
down into unseen coolness.
The well is deep.
Each morning I've time to fear
the water has sunk down into misty darkness,
and the chain will be swallowed by thirsty walls,
throat go dry,
heart shrink

pail hit bottom.

The valley

No-one took your hand and said:
take care.
This is now.
The valley with winding waters that you see
with deep woods and gentle air
with meadows and green springs
this valley bears the name of Love.

No-one said:
slow down.
Take care not to travel too fast,
to believe in another valley
a larger one you've heard of
there is no other
not for you
hold back
print each leaf in memory.

No-one said:
this is now.
This is a lot.
This is enough.

I ran through the valley all alone
not until I looked round did I realise:
that's how it looked.
That was it.

November

At last. The puddles are frozen together.
Stubble-fur stiff with every hair on end.
Frost has remembered every little fringe.
At last no more rush of despair,
darkness howling over itself.
Earth that just sighed and drooped
has hardened and raised its hackles at last:
the time has come for the naked
for clear dry boughs
for lingonberries' bitter drops of blood.
Earth has taken its reason captive:
a weather-beaten woman on the far side of her sex.

The wind

The wind doesn't wheedle now,
sniff round every bush
doesn't
curl itself up in clovery sun and sleep.
Doesn't sulk any more,
pull the birches' pigtails,
whip up the bay with a black stick
suddenly feel sorry
weep in a green strait
howl
around the chimney, scared of the dark.

The wind has grown up.
Seed-warm
it roars like a heavy sun
over the tree tops' heavenly meadow.

Doesn't need to knock down trees,
rape fluttering flowers.

Now it loves thousands of trees,
thousands of flowers,
blows its hayscent to the sea,
knows itself, has forgotten itself

fulfils its heart on its own
stronger
grizzled
salt.

Three sisters

The woman bent down to pick up her child
and her hair fell over her face
and inside her a little old woman
clear-eyed, dry
and doddery
bent down for her knitting
and inside her
a girl bent down for her doll
with gentle hands

three sisters
who would never see each other.

Portrait

When she deceived her husband she was still alive.
When she deceived her lover
she'd finally learned:
never give more than is asked of you.
She gets more and more beautiful, they said.
She's grown up now.
Carefully
under a rain of flowers
she carried the glass casket in her heart:
the little girl who could only give everything.

Take-off

The fuselage crouches
doesn't dare   doesn't dare
giving birth is dying
straight through the pain
the command's wilder roar
O God take it away —

the body draws breath again
breast shining with sweat

but the command throbs.
Howling with terror
wings rise into black gale
howling with joy
death hurls the body away

but the wings carry
the wings carry

this is no delivery
it's more
not the absence of pain
more:

shining circles of immensity.

So shall I rise
in circle after circle
break from my shell
the day I'm reborn.

from
Lower your lamp
(1963)

The birds

At first I heard only the voices
yours and mine
weaving around each other
some words fell behind us.
Later I heard the birds
weaving their nest of rain-threads
in the mist.
Wings shot down
behind us
beaks fought
over diamonds.

The cave

Such power the lovers had
to hurt each other.
They knew the entrance to each other's solitude
and the branches that hid the cave's mouth,
they knew how memory slinks darkly
along narrow corridors, knew plants
that paled at footsteps and where
rills broke out like tears.
They stooped down cautiously by the spring
outside the cave entrance, drank
clear presence of mind from a cupped hand,
pulled off their hard shoes and went in
with bare feet.

The star

Suddenly I pulled one arm free
from the arms that enclosed me
and stretched it out to touch a star:
yes, she was there, she hadn't changed colour,
the star was as deep as ever with blue points
and mine, only mine —
      the star was in her place
we smiled gently at each other
and we both turned round
      each to our heaven.

The pelican

Turned aside, on the nest's edge,
she preens sparse feathers.
What do the chicks care
if her breast
bears bloody streaks.

The poet's cave

The old poet was startled
he blinked timidly
outside the cave black suns
and spears whizzed by

they're playing with blood
those who've not yet bled to death
they invoke the devil
and dare a huge voice

the old poet fears words
he knows they must be paid for
with deadly reality

no smoke comes from his soul
it's light as ashes

he picks up tiny words
downy and warm as leaves
at the mouth of oblivion.

from
Scrapbook
(1968)

The song of the mouse

They burned down the witch's house.
Came with straw and stakes
curses and yells.
Spat on the ashes:
She can burn in hell.

No one saw the mouse.
It scurried away
among all the feet
silent, free.

Well away from the fire
sat down, sniffed the air: let's see,
where shall I build now:
Who shall I choose to be?

Conversation

They'd lived together forty years
and language grew harder and harder to understand.
To start with they'd managed a few words
later contented themselves with nods:
bed and board.
For forty years they'd coped with everyday usage
their faces grew blank, like stones.

But sometimes a chance interpreter came along:
a cat, an unusual sunset.
They listened with an air of disquiet
tried to answer
            but were already dumb.

The lads

Once they were big
sap tensed their skin
then they played, cocky and wicked,
but then their wives were wives

now they sit
with doddering necks
thin white hair
good little boys
and their mothers sit
with them broad, sheltering,
comforting them with their unawareness
of how once
when wives were wives

The hostess

In the end her dress grew so wide
you couldn't even see the tray she carried
the dress of thick warm air
with little labels pinned all over it
Come in! You're looking well!
      How's everything?
The hospitable air was so creamy
there were so many labels
she didn't need to talk
just carry things around.
She would hardly have recognised her own voice
a tiny voice screaming
I don't want to! Go away!

Later

Later when God had flickered out on all the branches
the human being stood there
a Christmas tree with needles shed
looked around in daylight
and dimly remembered
something that had made her shine.

from
The four flute players
(1975)

Sea in November

Around the house, quiet under the trees
sit big transparent figures
they don't bar the way
you can walk right through them
only a slight chill
but they're always there
easier to see in wet weather
when the sea is grey
when what has been rises up
towards the window.

Winter beach

Calm had already descended
and the little clear mirrors finally joined up
to make a continent.
The whipped straws of the beach were captured
motionless, in fists of ice.
But this was towards evening.
We hadn't wished for what happened in the night
we thought we had weathered the storm.
Heavily and slowly the whole sea rocked
and in dark pieces the calm broke up.

This you and me

This you and me
this us.
That it can last.
Sometimes it takes shape
like an object I weigh in my hand
so firm and warm I can taste, see
what we share
as indispensable
as bread and salt.

Portrait of a raspberry

Just as raspberry runners travel under the sand
and put out new shoots each year
       he had travelled
far from his beginnings, had forgotten
and since he only lived in his outpost,
his remotest rootlet, thought he was new
and singular to the species.
       If he'd turned round
he'd have seen similar bushes the whole way:
even in the mother-bush the one he was.

Cat's evening

Long ago they'd stopped caressing each other
but their hands had stored up warmth
and the cat's fur grew sleeker
smooth and glossy.
At evening the cat went from lap to lap
purring with sheathed claws.

The dolls

But when she looked at all those years
they'd turned into dolls, with glassy eyes
some dozing, some wide awake
some splendidly dressed, with bouffant hair
some naked, with breasts and slender arms
none able to move, all in a row
      she stuffed them into a sack and
            pulled its string tight
now they've gone
      now they've really gone

The moment

The moment the shutters are nailed up
the hammering stops
when friends have gone away
and the grass has already forgotten

the four flute players arise
from the corners where they'd been sitting
                                    invisible.

Sorrow

Now sorrow has claimed this headland too
now I can never go there again and breathe
now the heedless waving reed says
now the sneaking blue vetch says
now the lonely spiraea says
and the little yellow stars
of the patient stonecrop tuft:
Here she walked.
Here she talked.

The stump

Nothing's as stubborn as hope,
nothing wilier, more wilful.
I look at the stump:
            maimed,
meek and dumb in the cold.
But:
the merest hint of thaw,
yes, even before,
and around the scars creep little shoots
foolhardy, green,
unabashed,
give me a deal of trouble
a deal of unnecessary joy

me and the blade.

All trees wait for birds

When light opens its eyes
the landscape is new-fallen snow
and fresh as frost
no tracks to be seen

not the faintest featherstitch of lies
the shadow's a hungry blue
and all trees wait for birds
all unknown
here is neither good nor bad
      a mouse
      scampers fearless across the sun.

Scent of apples

We who are left remember the old mothers
the scent of shrivelled apples
spectacles, listening, gleaming

grey plaits at night-time
bible on the bedside table
they never told us who they prayed for

we who are left saw the old mothers
worn out as their sheets
pin patch to patch
everything taken care of
sheets and people
nothing wasted

they never told us the mothers
how downtrodden they were
what they had hidden
their eyes were clear as little girls'
tidying their corner for the night
before slipping into bed.

Gone away

It's quite possible when you sit in the sun
to sit in the shade, see the rolling waves
merely as glinting lies over the rocks
only see hunger in gulls' yellow eyes
autumn in the sun-dried grass at your feet.
It's quite possible when you sit in the sun
to have gone away, not answer to a call
feel in your innermost room the grey hand
close the windows.

Siesta

Between three and four
I lie on my bed with bare feet
listen to the north-westerly in the TV aerial
between three and four, perfectly free
to choose my domain: to sleep through the roaring
or be changed, live like the gull
hover above the pine tree totally still
as if hung by a cord from the sun
regally choosing from among blue streets
between three and four
      perfectly free
to play the human, stretched out on a bed
or race with the gale
      over sparkling rocks.

from
**The sea sounds beyond
the trees**
(1980)

The forest stone

It's there all the time
although you don't see it.
The fir trees hide it,
under their grey mumble
rowan fingers
trace shifting shadows.
It's one with its forest.
But just before sunset
it comes into view
suddenly, wholly illumined:
heavy, its defiant peak
says: I'm here.
Sorrow does this too.

The sun's grave

This is the iron sea.
No sea for gentle ripples.
Nor for carefree sails.
Rust-red jaws
barely hidden
sharpest teeth
just under the keel.
This is the iron sea
without seaweed and small creatures.
This is the northern sea
used to hard against hard.

Every evening the sea gulps.
Fireball glows and hisses
rallies courage to go under.
This is the iron sea
that wants the cold.

The answer

Some time must have been the first time,
in an existence in another place
in another time lost to me now
I must have answered the question.
Why does it keep being asked?
Who was I once?
Who did I once betray?
Treachery is there too, a vague answer,
a memory from an inaccessible place
and I keep being given new chances
to give a new answer.

Close

The water in the well sinks
when the sea ebbs from the beach
always rises in the well
when the sea comes in again
so in the one the courage to live
rises and sinks
Each flowing like the other
when you're close.

The burning glass

As in spring
you catch the sun in a burning glass
watching the heat dwindle
and the paper blacken,
a tiny point in it
begin to glow,
surely that's how despair
should burn a hole in silence.

Joy

In the end she stopped trying to please
anyone except God or death, both far away,
allowed herself to be what she was
(and as he said)
an old bag.
Now she grew almost beautiful with relief,
let her hair and clothes go,
said what she liked.
After all, men were only small boys
someone had given birth to some time,
just troublesome and demanding.

Someone to remember with

You couldn't say he grieved.
He probably hardly remembered what she looked like
she'd been there pottering around so long
she seemed more like a hole in the air.
Still it was hard for him to forgive her
for taking fifty years away with her,
fifty years and more of his life
so there was no-one to tug at any more
and say: Remember?

Dismissed

I

Night-time, the hip's ridge lifts,
knee slides down over knee,
        he feels
the heavy skeleton within,
enigmatically him,
        he knows
what he'll part from one day
        — himself or not himself.
His skull is hard and hot,
a thing not even death
will crush, there's thought in there
and the one thinking is him.
How can he believe he'll cease
when everything that's kept him upright,
the faithful spine, the legs,
everything that will only be visible
after he's gone,
when it steadfastly stops
        — himself or not himself.

II

It must have happened to a stranger.
It never ceased to surprise him
that it happened without his leave,
that his body was quietly preparing something
        or wasn't it his blood
        his lungs   his heart
        did they belong to someone else
        who had never made himself known
        but had just been there
        and by whose mercy he'd lived,
someone he couldn't thank
for the long liaison
and not even ask
if he'd been dismissed
        and from what date.

III

They said: he's in his second childhood.
Yes, there was childhood in his speech,

so important it was to recall the beginning:
hit on a memory, perfectly fresh
never worn out:
ray of sunlight on a kitchen floor
the knotted edge of the rag rug
voices over his head,
hit on a self, a totally unused self
before it ran off and was lost,
grown up, or matured, but lost
in what they called an active life
that was now unreal and misty.
The security of recognising
the worn threshold:
he saw himself stand
with the wind in his hair
he saw how the maple in the yard
rocked stars
far away, deep and near.
They said: he's lost himself
but he had found
he had completed the circle.

IV
So long as he knows
it's he who forgets
and trips and stumbles
and mumbles at his stick

so long as it's he
who catches sight of himself through clouds
of drifting worn years
that he doesn't recognise

so long as he's there
in the face that changes

so long as he knows
who rises in his eyes
and calls from his gaze
when no one understands his mouth

so long as

November

Now life and death have gone their separate ways.
Death is still strolling
along the black leaves.
Life has gone home
to sleep in its roots.
The fields breathe deeply
and settle themselves.
Darkness and rest.   At last.

Winter tree

The tree's finest thoughts
are reserved for the frost
hardly conscious before
they're clearly defined
when they rise from the crown
when they fork outwards
more brittle and white
the closer to sky.
Nothing hidden
not even birds
only the bare trunk
dark and real.

Five-finger exercise

A snowy Sunday. Silence. Some mute flakes,
a hesitant glow behind treetrunks.
Silence and emptiness. Barely expectancy,
just five-finger exercises on the typewriter.
A friend who died but was never vanquished
once said: If you sit among your papers
they'll come to life, you'll find your way again.
Back again? Is it sure? But who to?

You knew the terms, you who died.
Life becomes more and more taking up room,
time to reflect, stepping aside.
It's a matter of taking out what's inside you,
what's accumulated down the years,
of being able to endure what's all too much,
what you can't acknowledge yet know.
I'm reminded of a great mountain, when you walked
                                   round it
it kept changing shape, different shadows
revealed new outcrops, hidden chasms,
and yet the damned thing was always the same.
What's the good of seeing how and why
from new angles and how sun and cloud
shift from clear view to twilight memory,
the mountain's there and it was yours.
And no one ever asks what you think
Of what was once you. It just is.

Outside snowflakes fall, thickening
only to hide away. But I shan't hide anything.
No, (although it's merely a five-finger exercise)
I'll invite home a few truths.

It's not so much what they'll say,
faced with a calm and merciless magnifier
I've already made the admissions; yes, I've done that
and worse things I wasn't even aware of, but
it couldn't have happened any other way,

it was predestined, so had to happen,
the way I was and others were then
(and yet: hard to forgive yourself
                          — and the others).

Yet it's far worse when the truths keep silent,
turn aside as if in scorn,
cloak themselves in clouds and blur the view.
I ask: Was it like that? Was it really like that?
I only want to discover the truth,
whether I lied to myself or to others.
And I'm not afraid.
                          But no one answers.
Whatever happened is none of their concern.

That's what's worst of all: being left alone
with silent places hidden within you
and to see them rising up out of your dreams
twisted, strange, in a distorted light
with secret messages from that underworld
where it's all buried —
                          But before it's time to go
I have to acknowledge myself fully,
before abandoning myself to oblivion
with 'thanks for the loan'. No day
empty, and in vain.
                          Silence. Snowflakes fall
and what happens now is just a re-echo
of all that's gone before through snow and summers
and perhaps is happening just when nothing happens
while I'm tapping out my five-finger exercise.

from
The waterwheel
(1986)

The palimpsest

All of it must fit on a scrap of parchment
I keep with me always, surprised that
the writing's grown hard to make out.
A later script runs across the first
and over that another, fine and fleeting
some rubbed away, some crossed out.
What happened last can still be read
but how to get at earlier signs
and will the palimpsest hold any more?

Together with time

One day the door of my room was closed
and fate told me: be still.
It was then I discovered time.
It had lain hidden under a lid
of events and hasty decisions.
It was then I lifted the lid.
So strange! Time was really there
quite unused, quite itself,
smooth and fresh, as if resting.
I looked at time with reverence.
Saw myself anew, sank into
a wondrous eventlessness
together with time
listened to myself living:
a barely perceptible murmur.

The waterwheel

The ox plods heavily with blindfold eyes,
the wheel turns slowly, relentlessly,
creates time, a thing not visible
which actually is nothing
      with a licence to kill.

The north buoy

The north buoy lies askew in the Sound, slants
its red basket over ripples of glitter, dances
in fair winds, gulls lime the basket,
algae twine the pole, sand eels jump.
The north buoy idles and plays.
       Next morning
the wind has changed, grown surly
force 6, the buoy tugs and rocks,
drags, askew in the other direction.
Renegade, we say, sitter on the fence!
Look how the buoy plunges, will soon blow away!
No, no danger for the buoy, it merely studies
wind and current, only seems to obey.
The pole stays firmly fastened to the weight below.

Scratching tree

Just as the cat stretches itself each morning
and sharpens its claws on the same stump
I have my scratching tree, an obstinate poem
with deepcut scorings where time after time
I tear out hackneyed words and try out new.
Not a rejected, not a discarded poem,
on the contrary, one most dear to me
but stubborn, it wants heavy sluggish words
and stubborn, I want fresher crisper ones.
We keep at it, we fight our lengthy duel.
I hone my claws on my sulky scratching tree.

Snowy evening

In this landscape silence has cloaked all tracks
trees are thinned out to graphite-grey streaks
left-behind leaves are thin nets of nerves
the stars mere pinpricks
          don't go out
you'll be like me, struck dumb.

The spruce tree

I met it one evening. Out of the dark snow
rose the giant spruce tree, blocked my way
with something that was more than icy silence,
it was a black, almost audible threat.
And there was nobody who could translate
the spruce's gruff speech into human tongue.
I was an intruder, a nobody to the spruce.
It stood scornful, rooted in its ice-age,
an older form of life.

Frau Bach

Now and then she forgot him altogether
in a sweaty tangle of chores
one day when he lingered at the organ maybe
building, as he said, a cathedral of order
or on a day filled with servant-girls' clatter
frying smells and tankards or when small heels
kicked hard under her dress.
Now and then she forgot the weighty precentor
for what he had given her to endure,
    disappointments too,
princely disfavour, his gloomy silence,
he seemed hardly to notice all those children
except at table, she pulled Friedemann's hair,
he tapped out a fugue with his soupspoon,
she was fully occupied keeping order
but sometimes she recalled:
    how one hectic day just before Christmas
    before the Lord's coming which required
        so much food,
    she had leaned her brow against the frozen pane:
    a moment's rest in the ice crystals' order.

Käthe Kollwitz

Just before she became *entartet**
the critic sought her out,
it was hard enough to find the way
to her husband, the poor folks' doctor,
in the hungry Berlin district
but worse on the staircase,
coughing, shuffling old codgers,
and he was almost knocked down
by the old woman with the crutch.
He never managed to ask
where she found the mood of her woodcuts,
her lines of deep suffering.
He saw her at the top of the stairs,
skinny kids clutching at her,
their eyes like holes in hard shells,
(they'd have millions of siblings later)
he recognised them from her prints,
recognised her, herself,
broad and angry, sweat on her brow,
dressed in tenderness and an old frock,
her whole being in action
but when could she have time to —
he heard her shout up there:
Gehen Sie weg! ich habe nie Zeit!

*Hitler's term for degenerate

from
A way to
measure time
(1989)

The minute

It could happen to him anywhere at all,
in the bus, in the street, amid crowds,
that he was set free from the hurly-burly,
slipped through an invisible chink
and swam out into an ocean of time.
He could swim whichever way he liked,
back into time past
or on by an unmarked route
where no one was waiting, a boundless time
enveloping him like clear water.
He was washed ashore by that minute.

Sun-memory

Fossil resin, a scrap of trapped sunshine
dark as honey and light
one day three million years ago
in the tropical northern forests
it slid down a pine trunk
and dragged with it a little seed,
the tender seed-wing flies
imprisoned in sunshine.

Fallen nest

A nest fallen to earth, he picked it up:
network of patience
woven with delicate twigs
lined with soft breast feathers
caulked with down.
The nest, warm with summer
fresh with breezy sunshine
— and he, an old man,
buried his face in the forgotten scent
sharply aware of loss —
the downy years.

The cradle

From the northern ocean
at the end of the tenth month
she set out to find a warmer home,
taking her soundings from the moving coast,
spiralling the great spool
down through silent purple-blue layers
lit faintly from above
spiralling grey as graphite
down towards the dimmer room
where only little fish could slip through the walls.
There no one could get at her precious only child,
there they could rock flank to flank,
from where they would rise together,
fill their lungs with sun and sink again
down to the sea's nursery depths.

Sea-day

We rowed home at evening
　　rowed with dripping oars
while a fiery-red orb
　　touched the sea's rim
the rock with its stored warmth
　　quivered, doubled in the deep,
pike, rod and reel
　　side by side on our thwart.
Then a head rose up
　　in the stern's bright furrow
with dripping moustache
　　his head rose and fell,
his old wise eyes
　　pensively regarding
us who had plundered his store-pot,
　　us who had borrowed his sea.

Twilight

He was hurrying too much, whoever it was passed by.
The old woman, in the twilight, in her long dress
tidies up after the scythe, snapped stalks,
torn leaves, the wing of a fledgling,
she mumbles, gathers into her old hand
what life has hurt and maimed and left behind.
Her dress is ample, her pockets full.

Ett sätt att räkna tiden

Ett vingslag blixtrade vid grottans mynning
och solens avsked var en klargrön tuva
när vi sjönk ner och mörkret svalde oss.
Vi kröp i fuktiga och trånga gångar
där bara kylan andades, och plötsligt
stod vi upprätta i en väldig sal
där taket lyftes dunkelt utom synhåll
och ekot löpte ifrån vägg till vägg
förvillande, mångfaldigt, som om röster
från någon bortglömd tid bevarats
och frusits in i grottans akustik.
I klasar hängde takets tunga frukter
och droppade sedan miljoner år
sin våta kalk, ett sätt att räkna tiden.
Vi lyste på dem, mörknat midnattsblå
och röda som av flådda bisonkroppar.
Här bodde folk för sextitusen år sen
sa guiden, och däruppe är en öppning
till nästa grotta, då var mänskan vig
och kunde klättra, hundratusen år sen.
Då såg vi medan guiden stod och talte
ett annat folk, det allra äldsta folket.
Det kröp ihop i sina våta mantlar
och krökte sina nackar under taket
där sedan tidens början droppar fallit
och där det vuxit till för varje droppe.
Det var ett tystlåtet och tåligt folk
som mindes mest, som gömde sina minnen
och vände värdigt ryggarna åt oss
inkränglingar och flyktiga som nuet.

A way to measure time

A wingbeat flashed outside the cave mouth
and the sun's departure was a clear green hillock
as we sank down, swallowed by the darkness.
We crept along damp and narrow passageways
where only chillness breathed, and suddenly
we could stand upright in a lofty chamber
whose ceiling rose up dimly out of sight
and echoes travelled on from wall to wall
confusingly, as if a multitude
of voices from some forgotten time were embalmed
seemingly frozen into the cave's acoustics.
The ceiling's heavy fruit hung in clusters
that through millions of years had been dripping
their liquid lime, a way to measure time.
We shone light on them, dark midnight blue
and red that seemed like flayed bison bodies.
Here sixty thousand years ago lived folk,
our guide said, up there you see a cleft
into the next cave, then people were agile,
could climb, a hundred thousand years ago.
Then as the guide was talking we could see
other people, the most ancient race.
They huddled close together in wet cloaks
and bowed their necks under the low roof
that since the start of time had been dripping
and with each single drop had been growing.
They were a taciturn and hardy folk
who remembered most, cherished their memories
and turned their backs on us with dignity,
intruders and as fleeting as the present.

Other Titles from
FOREST BOOKS

Special Collection

THE NAKED MACHINE Selected poems of Matthías Johannessen.
Translated from the *Icelandic* by Marshall Brement.
(Forest/Almenna bokáfélagid)
0 948259 44 2 cloth £7.95   0 948259 43 4 paper £5.95
96 pages. Illustrated

ON THE CUTTING EDGE Selected poems of Justo Jorge Padrón.
Translated from the *Spanish* by Louis Bourne.
0 948259 42 6 paper £7.95   176 pages

ROOM WITHOUT WALLS Selected poems of Bo Carpelan.
Translated from the *Swedish* by Anne Born.
0 948259 08 6 paper £6.95   144 pages. Illustrated

CALL YOURSELF ALIVE? The love poems of Nina Cassian.
Translated from the *Romanian* by Andrea Deletant and
Brenda Walker. Introduction by Fleur Adcock.
0 948259 38 8 paper £5.95.   96 pages. Illustrated

RUNNING TO THE SHROUDS Six sea stories of Konstantin
Stanyukovich. Translated from the *Russian* by Neil Parsons.
0 948259 06 X paper £5.95   112 pages.

A VANISHING EMPTINESS Selected poems of Willem M. Roggeman.
Edited by Yann Lovelock. Translated from the *Dutch*.
0 948259 51 5 £7.95   112 pages. Illustrated

PORTRAIT OF THE ARTIST AS AN ABOMINABLE SNOWMAN
Selected poems of Gabriel Rosenstock translated from the
Irish by Michael Hartnett. New Poems translated by Jason
Sommer. Dual text.
0 948259 56 6 paper £7.95   112 pages

LAND AND PEACE Selected poems of Desmond Egan translated
into Irish by Michael Hartnett. Gabriel Rosenstock, Douglas
Sealey and Tomas MacSiomoin. Dual text.
0 948259 64 7 paper £7.95   112 pages

THE EYE IN THE MIRROR Selected poems of Takis Varvitsiotis.
Translated from the *Greek* by Kimon Friar. (Forest/Paratiritis)
0 948259 59 0 paper £8.95   160 pages

THE WORLD AS IF Selected poems of Uffe Harder.
Translated from the *Danish* by John F. Deane and Uffe Harder.
Forest/Dedalus.
0 948259 76 0 paper £4.95   80 pages

SPRINGTIDES Selected poems of Pia Tafdrup.
Translated from the *Danish* by Anne Born.
0 948259 55 8 paper £6.95   96 pages

HEARTWORK Stories of Solveig von Schoultz.
Translated from *Finland/Swedish* by Marlaine Delargy and
Joan Tate. Introduction by Bo Carpelan.
0 948259 50 7 paper £7.95   128 pages

THICKHEAD AND OTHER STORIES by Haldun Taner.
Translated from the *Turkish* by Geoffrey Lewis.
UNESCO collection of representative works.
0 948259 58 2 paper £8.95   176 pages

East European Series

FOOTPRINTS OF THE WIND Selected poems of Mateja Matevski.
Translated from the *Macedonian* by Ewald Osers.
Introduction by Robin Skelton. Arts Council funded.
0 948259 41 8 paper £6.95   96 pages. Illustrated

ARIADNE'S THREAD An anthology of contemporary Polish
women poets. Translated from the *Polish* by Susan Bassnett and
Piotr Kuhiwczak. UNESCO collection of representative works.
0 948259 45 0 paper £6.95   96 pages

POETS OF BULGARIA An anthology of contemporary Bulgarian poets.
Edited by William Meredith. Introduction by Alan Brownjohn.
0 948259 39 6 paper £6.95   112 pages

FIRES OF THE SUNFLOWER Selected poems by Ivan Davidkov.
Translated from the *Bulgarian* by Ewald Osers.
0 948259 48 5 paper £6.95   96 pages. Illustrated

STOLEN FIRE Selected poems by Lyubomir Levchev.
Translated from the *Bulgarian* by Ewald Osers.
Introduction by John Balaban.
UNESCO collection of representative works.
0 948259 04 3 paper £5.95   112 pages. Illustrated

AN ANTHOLOGY OF CONTEMPORARY ROMANIAN POETRY
Translated by Andrea Deletant and Brenda Walker.
0 9509487 4 8 paper £5.00   112 pages.

GATES OF THE MOMENT Selected poems of Ion Stoica.
Translated from the *Romanian* by Brenda Walker and
Andrea Deletant. Dual text with cassette.
0 9509487 0 5 paper £5.00   126 pages
Cassette £3.50 plus VAT

SILENT VOICES An anthology of contemporary Romanian women
poets. Translated by Andrea Deletant and Brenda Walker.
0 948259 03 5 paper £6.95   172 pages

EXILE ON A PEPPERCORN Selected poems of Mircea Dinescu.
Translated from the *Romanian* by Andrea Deletant and
Brenda Walker.
0 948259 00 0 paper £5.95   96 pages. Illustrated

LET'S TALK ABOUT THE WEATHER Selected poems of Marin Sorescu
Translated from the *Romanian* by Andrea Deletant and
Brenda Walker.
0 9509487 8 0 paper £5.95   96 pages

THE THIRST OF THE SALT MOUNTAIN Three plays by Marin Sorescu
(Jonah, The Verger, and the Matrix)
Translated from the *Romanian* by Andrea Deletant and
Brenda Walker.
0 9509487 5 6 paper £6.95   124 pages. Illustrated

VLAD DRACULA THE IMPALER A play by Marin Sorescu
Translated from the *Romanian* by Dennis Deletant.
0 948259 07 8 paper £6.95   112 pages. Illustrated

THE ROAD TO FREEDOM Poems and Prose Poems by Geo Milev
Translated from the *Bulgarian* by Ewald Osers.
0 948259 40 X paper £6.95   96 pages

IN CELEBRATION OF MIHAI EMINESCU Selected poems and extracts
translated from the *Romanian* by Brenda Walker and
Horia Florian Popescu. Illustrated by Sabin Balaşa.
0 948259 62 0 cloth £20. Limited Edition.   176 pages.

THROUGH THE NEEDLE'S EYE Selected poems of Jon Milos.
Translated from the *Romanian* by Brenda Walker and Jon Milos.
0 948259 61 2 paper £6.95   96 pages.

YOUTH WITHOUT YOUTH and other Novellas by Mircea Eliade.
Edited and with an introduction by Matei Calinescu.
Translated from the *Romanian* by MacLinscott Ricketts.
0 948259 74 4 paper £12.95   328 pages

A WOMAN'S HEART Stories by Jordan Yovkov.
Translated from the *Bulgarian* by John Burnip.
0 948259 54 X paper £9.95   208 pages